T0078141

WORLD WAR III

MOVING NOW

Christian Wilhelm Florenes

authorHOUSE®

AuthorHouse™
1663 Liberty Drive
Bloomington, IN 47403
www.authorhouse.com
Phone: 1 (800) 839-8640

Published by AuthorHouse 11/20/2015

ISBN: 978-1-5049-6180-6 (sc)
ISBN: 978-1-5049-6179-0 (e)

Library of Congress Control Number: 2015919452

Print information available on the last page.

Any people depicted in stock imagery provided by Thinkstock are models, and such images are being used for illustrative purposes only. Certain stock imagery © Thinkstock.

This book is printed on acid-free paper.

Because of the dynamic nature of the Internet, any web addresses or links contained in this book may have changed since publication and may no longer be valid. The views expressed in this work are solely those of the author and do not necessarily reflect the views of the publisher, and the publisher hereby disclaims any responsibility for them.

DEDICATION

I dedicate this work to my dreams which have always offered love and support and have always been there for me. Thank you so much.

Christian Wilhelm Florenes

A message of very important information is in this book. The author will tell about the coming war that may be a huge catastrophe in the world, particularly Europe and Asia. The writer has received many incredible dreams about what might happen. The author will write some short and simple points and their purpose is to help readers take care of this serious message.

Christian is a non-religious and active man who is 42 years old. He is interested in learning between earth and heaven and in learning a lot about signs of animal communication. Animals are really valuable for people. Moreover, he loves the outdoors, sports, playing golf and traveling abroad.

Christian Wilhelm Florenes

When I was very young, I cannot remember what age exactly I was, but I remember very well when I got some weird thoughts in my head. They told me that Russia was a threat to Norway. My father said that the US and the NATO military defended Norway. Then I stopped thinking about this.

When I was in the United States to study
in university, I met some interesting
people who talked about the Earth, heaven,
and in between as well as predictions
of World War 3, etc... In the United
States, I began to study books to figure
out when the war might commence.
A very famous fortuneteller named
Nostradamus had many predictions
come true. One of those predictions
mentioned World War 3. But I did
not find any correct timings.

Meanwhile, I've got a number
of strange dreams that I could
remember well when I woke up.

A dream has said that I am going to
know exactly when the war begins.
What are dreams? All people dream
in different ways. Most of them have
learned that dreams are fantasies. When
you believe in your dreams, they will
give you exciting messages and signals.
How can one remember dreams? You
might say to yourself that you will try
to apprehend upcoming dreams. These
dreams can give you some nice threads.
Here I shall not elaborate further.

An unique dream sent a message to me in the night and when I woke up I was in a shock. It said that I was going to get the exact time when war comes. Many dreams have instructed me smoothly. They do not come daily. Sometimes dreams explain what might happen before, during, and after the war. Readers can hear more about dream indications from the next page on.

First, one of the dreams mentioned that I must share this incredibly important message. So that people can prepare themselves before the war happens. Moreover, I must inform of that issue in good time, avoiding shock or unpreparedness. After people read the book, they will probably prepare well.

Previously, I have tried to give lectures and talk to everyone, but it did not help because of Janteloven and Social Democrats in Europe. Most people have not believed what I have ever said. My first lecture (the picture on the previous page) was posted for five years. Finally, I am taking a chance and publishing this book. This book is my debut. I do not expect to write beautiful language, but publish significant content.

A little review of the history
about World War 2.

Hitler began to gain power in 1930
Czechoslovakia and Austria were
invaded by Germany in 1939
War was declared when Poland was
attacked by Germany in the same year.
Norway was attacked on April 9, 1940.
The war lasted for 5-6years.

Dreams characterize Russia as the greatest threat to the world. They have invested heavily in military development and spent frantic mass billions to improve the professional military.

The second biggest threat is China. The Russian military is allied with China. The alliance will be the greatest threat to the world. China has also invested in its military.

How does the war start?

It can be caused by a small conflict.

When does the war begin?

The war could be begin in about <u>1-2</u> years.
Dreams never provide precise figures.
It is said that it will be very soon.

Perviously, Russia invaded two states in Georgia for just a few days and occupied a part of eastern Ukraine. Today, Russian planes are bombing Syria. It appears that Russia is using this as training. China has been a threat to other countries in Asia, especially via sea.

What will be the next target for Russia?

Russia will take the rest of Ukraine, Georgia and the former Soviet Union. Afterwards, the alliance will invade Europe.

What will be the target for China?

China will invade Japan, Taiwan
and possibly other countries.

What will happen during the war?

Atomic warfare will be used and one
part eight of the land in the world will be
crushed and destroyed. Nuclear weapons
will be an extreme threat in the world
and to human beings. People will have
to stay in their cellars without smelling
fresh air going into three weeks if a bomb
is exploded, it says in my dreams.

The writer has dreamed that bombs
will be exploded in sea and air.
Coasts will be attacked after bombs
are exploded over the sea.

GERMANY

All European countries

Germany

The north of Germany will be bombed
from the east coast to the west coast.

Civilians

Innocent civilians will be killed.
Known people and children are made
human shields and will be killed
by soldiers. Women are raped.

History has shown that Russian soldiers
often rape. However, the writer´s
dreams warn that Chinese soldiers
behave worse than the Russians.

Safety

Dreams characterize the United States, Canada and Tenerife as safe and secure places. People can stay there for a few years until the war is over and move back when countries are recovered. Recommend moving to safe countries as soon as possible, preferably before the war starts.

Safety Part 2

People can begin to visit anywhere in these countries and prepare for whichever country they wish to live in. They should start to look for work now. Maybe readers have family or friends they can stay with. It is recommended that you do that now. It might be challenging to act on and you might meet a lot of doubt. But it is valuable for human life.

The alliance will design a new symbol
for their flag. Many small stars
and one hammer, like a communist
symbol, are on the flag. It seems that
the color of the background is red.

Norway

The country will be in a complex situation when Russian and Chinese military attacks. The norwegian military will lose the game because Norwegians weapon equiement will be out bottom and Norwegian military is powerless.

Contact:
www.elglenger.com
email: mail@elglenger.com

The author would like to try to respond
to questions but will be unable to
answer some questions. Some of these,
readers must resolve by themselves.

Dear Readers!

I wish that readers continue on a successful
path and thank you a lot for reading the
author's book. Hope that the book has
given some great advice to readers.
ADVICE FROM THE WRITER.
IT WOULD BE A WONDERFUL
HAPPENING IF READERS WOULD LIKE
TO SHARE SIGNIFICANT MESSAGES
WITH OTHER PEOPLE NOW.

Greetings,
Christian

The writer would like to share his latest nightly dreams with readers. These dreams would give more information about what would happen with World War 3.

Acknowlegdement

I would like to thank all to my friend, Louise Stern, who helped and advised me on this book project. Without her, I would not be able to do this project.

Moving now

Before the book is published, the writer has gotten his last dream that he has to add words "moving now" under the topic. The writer interpreters that the time will be very soon and serious and people have to move to one of the safe countries as soon as possible.

Printed in the United States
By Bookmasters